High J Strength & Conditioning Log

This Book Belongs To:

_____

DATE: | **WEEK:** | **WEIGHT:**

Warm Up/ Stretching				Duration:		

Exercise		Set 1	Set 2	Set 3	Set 4	Set 5
	Weight					
	Reps					
	Weight					
	Reps					
	Weight					
	Reps					
	Weight					
	Reps					
	Weight					
	Reps					
	Weight					
	Reps					
	Weight					
	Reps					
	Weight					
	Reps					
	Weight					
	Reps					
	Weight					
	Reps					
	Weight					
	Reps					
	Weight					
	Reps					
	Weight					
	Reps					

CARDIO WORKOUT

Exercise	Duration	Pace	Heart Rate	Calories

WATER 1 cup per circle
(1 cup = 8 ounces ~ 240ml)   ○○○○○○○○○○○○○○○○○○○○

DATE:	WEEK:	WEIGHT:

Warm Up/ Stretching	Duration:

Exercise		Set 1	Set 2	Set 3	Set 4	Set 5
	Weight					
	Reps					
	Weight					
	Reps					
	Weight					
	Reps					
	Weight					
	Reps					
	Weight					
	Reps					
	Weight					
	Reps					
	Weight					
	Reps					
	Weight					
	Reps					
	Weight					
	Reps					
	Weight					
	Reps					
	Weight					
	Reps					
	Weight					
	Reps					

CARDIO WORKOUT

Exercise	Duration	Pace	Heart Rate	Calories

WATER   1 cup per circle
(1 cup = 8 ounces ~ 240ml)   ◯◯◯◯◯◯◯◯◯◯◯◯◯◯◯◯

DATE:	WEEK:	WEIGHT:

Warm Up/ Stretching	Duration:

Exercise		Set 1	Set 2	Set 3	Set 4	Set 5
	Weight					
	Reps					
	Weight					
	Reps					
	Weight					
	Reps					
	Weight					
	Reps					
	Weight					
	Reps					
	Weight					
	Reps					
	Weight					
	Reps					
	Weight					
	Reps					
	Weight					
	Reps					
	Weight					
	Reps					
	Weight					
	Reps					
	Weight					
	Reps					
	Weight					
	Reps					

CARDIO WORKOUT

Exercise	Duration	Pace	Heart Rate	Calories

WATER   1 cup per circle
(1 cup = 8 ounces ~ 240ml)   ○○○○○○○○○○○○○○○○

DATE:	WEEK:	WEIGHT:

Warm Up/ Stretching	Duration:

Exercise		Set 1	Set 2	Set 3	Set 4	Set 5
	Weight					
	Reps					
	Weight					
	Reps					
	Weight					
	Reps					
	Weight					
	Reps					
	Weight					
	Reps					
	Weight					
	Reps					
	Weight					
	Reps					
	Weight					
	Reps					
	Weight					
	Reps					
	Weight					
	Reps					
	Weight					
	Reps					
	Weight					
	Reps					

CARDIO WORKOUT

Exercise	Duration	Pace	Heart Rate	Calories

WATER   1 cup per circle
(1 cup = 8 ounces ~ 240ml)   ○○○○○○○○○○○○○○○○○○

DATE:		WEEK:		WEIGHT:	

Warm Up/ Stretching			Duration:	

Exercise		Set 1	Set 2	Set 3	Set 4	Set 5
	Weight					
	Reps					
	Weight					
	Reps					
	Weight					
	Reps					
	Weight					
	Reps					
	Weight					
	Reps					
	Weight					
	Reps					
	Weight					
	Reps					
	Weight					
	Reps					
	Weight					
	Reps					
	Weight					
	Reps					
	Weight					
	Reps					
	Weight					
	Reps					

CARDIO WORKOUT

Exercise	Duration	Pace	Heart Rate	Calories

WATER   1 cup per circle
(1 cup = 8 ounces ~ 240ml)   ○○○○○○○○○○○○○○○○○○

DATE:		WEEK:		WEIGHT:	

Warm Up/ Stretching Duration:

Exercise		Set 1	Set 2	Set 3	Set 4	Set 5
	Weight					
	Reps					
	Weight					
	Reps					
	Weight					
	Reps					
	Weight					
	Reps					
	Weight					
	Reps					
	Weight					
	Reps					
	Weight					
	Reps					
	Weight					
	Reps					
	Weight					
	Reps					
	Weight					
	Reps					
	Weight					
	Reps					
	Weight					
	Reps					

CARDIO WORKOUT

Exercise	Duration	Pace	Heart Rate	Calories

WATER   1 cup per circle
(1 cup = 8 ounces ~ 240ml)   ○○○○○○○○○○○○○○○○

DATE: | **WEEK:** | **WEIGHT:**

Warm Up/ Stretching				Duration:		

Exercise		Set 1	Set 2	Set 3	Set 4	Set 5
	Weight					
	Reps					
	Weight					
	Reps					
	Weight					
	Reps					
	Weight					
	Reps					
	Weight					
	Reps					
	Weight					
	Reps					
	Weight					
	Reps					
	Weight					
	Reps					
	Weight					
	Reps					
	Weight					
	Reps					
	Weight					
	Reps					
	Weight					
	Reps					
	Weight					
	Reps					

CARDIO WORKOUT

Exercise	Duration	Pace	Heart Rate	Calories

WATER   1 cup per circle
(1 cup = 8 ounces ~ 240ml)   ○○○○○○○○○○○○○○○○○○

DATE:		WEEK:		WEIGHT:	

Warm Up/ Stretching	Duration:

Exercise		Set 1	Set 2	Set 3	Set 4	Set 5
	Weight					
	Reps					
	Weight					
	Reps					
	Weight					
	Reps					
	Weight					
	Reps					
	Weight					
	Reps					
	Weight					
	Reps					
	Weight					
	Reps					
	Weight					
	Reps					
	Weight					
	Reps					
	Weight					
	Reps					
	Weight					
	Reps					
	Weight					
	Reps					

CARDIO WORKOUT

Exercise	Duration	Pace	Heart Rate	Calories

WATER   1 cup per circle
(1 cup = 8 ounces ~ 240ml)   ○○○○○○○○○○○○○○○○○○

DATE:		WEEK:		WEIGHT:	

Warm Up/ Stretching   **Duration:**

Exercise		Set 1	Set 2	Set 3	Set 4	Set 5
	Weight					
	Reps					
	Weight					
	Reps					
	Weight					
	Reps					
	Weight					
	Reps					
	Weight					
	Reps					
	Weight					
	Reps					
	Weight					
	Reps					
	Weight					
	Reps					
	Weight					
	Reps					
	Weight					
	Reps					
	Weight					
	Reps					
	Weight					
	Reps					

CARDIO WORKOUT

Exercise	Duration	Pace	Heart Rate	Calories

WATER   1 cup per circle
(1 cup = 8 ounces ~ 240ml)   ○○○○○○○○○○○○○○○○○○

DATE:	WEEK:	WEIGHT:

Warm Up/ Stretching		Duration:

Exercise		Set 1	Set 2	Set 3	Set 4	Set 5
	Weight					
	Reps					
	Weight					
	Reps					
	Weight					
	Reps					
	Weight					
	Reps					
	Weight					
	Reps					
	Weight					
	Reps					
	Weight					
	Reps					
	Weight					
	Reps					
	Weight					
	Reps					
	Weight					
	Reps					
	Weight					
	Reps					
	Weight					
	Reps					

CARDIO WORKOUT

Exercise	Duration	Pace	Heart Rate	Calories

WATER   1 cup per circle
(1 cup = 8 ounces ~ 240ml)   ○ ○ ○ ○ ○ ○ ○ ○ ○ ○ ○ ○ ○ ○ ○ ○

DATE: **WEEK:**   **WEIGHT:**

Warm Up/ Stretching						**Duration:**

Exercise		Set 1	Set 2	Set 3	Set 4	Set 5
	Weight					
	Reps					
	Weight					
	Reps					
	Weight					
	Reps					
	Weight					
	Reps					
	Weight					
	Reps					
	Weight					
	Reps					
	Weight					
	Reps					
	Weight					
	Reps					
	Weight					
	Reps					
	Weight					
	Reps					
	Weight					
	Reps					
	Weight					
	Reps					

CARDIO WORKOUT

Exercise	Duration	Pace	Heart Rate	Calories

WATER   1 cup per circle
(1 cup = 8 ounces ~ 240ml)   ○○○○○○○○○○○○○○○○○○○

DATE:		WEEK:		WEIGHT:	

Warm Up/ Stretching				Duration:	

Exercise		Set 1	Set 2	Set 3	Set 4	Set 5
	Weight					
	Reps					
	Weight					
	Reps					
	Weight					
	Reps					
	Weight					
	Reps					
	Weight					
	Reps					
	Weight					
	Reps					
	Weight					
	Reps					
	Weight					
	Reps					
	Weight					
	Reps					
	Weight					
	Reps					
	Weight					
	Reps					
	Weight					
	Reps					

CARDIO WORKOUT

Exercise	Duration	Pace	Heart Rate	Calories

WATER   1 cup per circle
(1 cup = 8 ounces ~ 240ml)   ○○○○○○○○○○○○○○○○○○

DATE:	WEEK:	WEIGHT:

Warm Up/ Stretching	Duration:

Exercise		Set 1	Set 2	Set 3	Set 4	Set 5
	Weight					
	Reps					
	Weight					
	Reps					
	Weight					
	Reps					
	Weight					
	Reps					
	Weight					
	Reps					
	Weight					
	Reps					
	Weight					
	Reps					
	Weight					
	Reps					
	Weight					
	Reps					
	Weight					
	Reps					
	Weight					
	Reps					
	Weight					
	Reps					

CARDIO WORKOUT

Exercise	Duration	Pace	Heart Rate	Calories

WATER   1 cup per circle
(1 cup = 8 ounces ~ 240ml)   ○○○○○○○○○○○○○○○○○○

DATE:		WEEK:		WEIGHT:	

Warm Up/ Stretching				Duration:	

Exercise		Set 1	Set 2	Set 3	Set 4	Set 5
	Weight					
	Reps					
	Weight					
	Reps					
	Weight					
	Reps					
	Weight					
	Reps					
	Weight					
	Reps					
	Weight					
	Reps					
	Weight					
	Reps					
	Weight					
	Reps					
	Weight					
	Reps					
	Weight					
	Reps					
	Weight					
	Reps					
	Weight					
	Reps					

CARDIO WORKOUT

Exercise	Duration	Pace	Heart Rate	Calories

WATER 1 cup per circle
(1 cup = 8 ounces ~ 240ml)   ○○○○○○○○○○○○○○○○

DATE: **WEEK:** **WEIGHT:**

Warm Up/ Stretching						**Duration:**	

Exercise		Set 1	Set 2	Set 3	Set 4	Set 5
	Weight					
	Reps					
	Weight					
	Reps					
	Weight					
	Reps					
	Weight					
	Reps					
	Weight					
	Reps					
	Weight					
	Reps					
	Weight					
	Reps					
	Weight					
	Reps					
	Weight					
	Reps					
	Weight					
	Reps					
	Weight					
	Reps					
	Weight					
	Reps					

CARDIO WORKOUT

Exercise	Duration	Pace	Heart Rate	Calories

WATER   1 cup per circle
(1 cup = 8 ounces ~ 240ml)   ○○○○○○○○○○○○○○○○○○

DATE:	WEEK:	WEIGHT:

Warm Up/ Stretching		Duration:

Exercise		Set 1	Set 2	Set 3	Set 4	Set 5
	Weight					
	Reps					
	Weight					
	Reps					
	Weight					
	Reps					
	Weight					
	Reps					
	Weight					
	Reps					
	Weight					
	Reps					
	Weight					
	Reps					
	Weight					
	Reps					
	Weight					
	Reps					
	Weight					
	Reps					
	Weight					
	Reps					
	Weight					
	Reps					

CARDIO WORKOUT

Exercise	Duration	Pace	Heart Rate	Calories

WATER 1 cup per circle
(1 cup = 8 ounces ~ 240ml)   ○○○○○○○○○○○○○○○○○

DATE:	WEEK:	WEIGHT:

Warm Up/ Stretching		Duration:

Exercise		Set 1	Set 2	Set 3	Set 4	Set 5
	Weight					
	Reps					
	Weight					
	Reps					
	Weight					
	Reps					
	Weight					
	Reps					
	Weight					
	Reps					
	Weight					
	Reps					
	Weight					
	Reps					
	Weight					
	Reps					
	Weight					
	Reps					
	Weight					
	Reps					
	Weight					
	Reps					
	Weight					
	Reps					

CARDIO WORKOUT

Exercise	Duration	Pace	Heart Rate	Calories

WATER   1 cup per circle
(1 cup = 8 ounces ~ 240ml)   ○ ○ ○ ○ ○ ○ ○ ○ ○ ○ ○ ○ ○ ○ ○ ○ ○ ○

DATE:		WEEK:		WEIGHT:	

Warm Up/ Stretching				Duration:	

Exercise		Set 1	Set 2	Set 3	Set 4	Set 5
	Weight					
	Reps					
	Weight					
	Reps					
	Weight					
	Reps					
	Weight					
	Reps					
	Weight					
	Reps					
	Weight					
	Reps					
	Weight					
	Reps					
	Weight					
	Reps					
	Weight					
	Reps					
	Weight					
	Reps					
	Weight					
	Reps					
	Weight					
	Reps					

CARDIO WORKOUT

Exercise	Duration	Pace	Heart Rate	Calories

WATER 1 cup per circle
(1 cup = 8 ounces ~ 240ml)   ○○○○○○○○○○○○○○○○○

DATE: | **WEEK:** | **WEIGHT:**

| Warm Up/ Stretching | | Duration: | |

Exercise		Set 1	Set 2	Set 3	Set 4	Set 5
	Weight					
	Reps					
	Weight					
	Reps					
	Weight					
	Reps					
	Weight					
	Reps					
	Weight					
	Reps					
	Weight					
	Reps					
	Weight					
	Reps					
	Weight					
	Reps					
	Weight					
	Reps					
	Weight					
	Reps					
	Weight					
	Reps					
	Weight					
	Reps					

CARDIO WORKOUT

Exercise	Duration	Pace	Heart Rate	Calories

WATER 1 cup per circle
(1 cup = 8 ounces ~ 240ml)   ○○○○○○○○○○○○○○○○○○○

DATE:		WEEK:		WEIGHT:	

Warm Up/ Stretching					Duration:	

Exercise		Set 1	Set 2	Set 3	Set 4	Set 5
	Weight					
	Reps					
	Weight					
	Reps					
	Weight					
	Reps					
	Weight					
	Reps					
	Weight					
	Reps					
	Weight					
	Reps					
	Weight					
	Reps					
	Weight					
	Reps					
	Weight					
	Reps					
	Weight					
	Reps					
	Weight					
	Reps					
	Weight					
	Reps					
	Weight					
	Reps					

CARDIO WORKOUT

Exercise	Duration	Pace	Heart Rate	Calories

WATER   1 cup per circle
(1 cup = 8 ounces ~ 240ml)   ○○○○○○○○○○○○○○○○○

DATE: _____ **WEEK:** _____ **WEIGHT:** _____

Warm Up/ Stretching			Duration:		

Exercise		Set 1	Set 2	Set 3	Set 4	Set 5
	Weight					
	Reps					
	Weight					
	Reps					
	Weight					
	Reps					
	Weight					
	Reps					
	Weight					
	Reps					
	Weight					
	Reps					
	Weight					
	Reps					
	Weight					
	Reps					
	Weight					
	Reps					
	Weight					
	Reps					
	Weight					
	Reps					
	Weight					
	Reps					

CARDIO WORKOUT

Exercise	Duration	Pace	Heart Rate	Calories

WATER   1 cup per circle
(1 cup = 8 ounces ~ 240ml)   ○○○○○○○○○○○○○○○○○○○

DATE:	WEEK:	WEIGHT:

Warm Up/ Stretching		Duration:

Exercise		Set 1	Set 2	Set 3	Set 4	Set 5
	Weight					
	Reps					
	Weight					
	Reps					
	Weight					
	Reps					
	Weight					
	Reps					
	Weight					
	Reps					
	Weight					
	Reps					
	Weight					
	Reps					
	Weight					
	Reps					
	Weight					
	Reps					
	Weight					
	Reps					
	Weight					
	Reps					
	Weight					
	Reps					

CARDIO WORKOUT

Exercise	Duration	Pace	Heart Rate	Calories

WATER 1 cup per circle
(1 cup = 8 ounces ~ 240ml) ○○○○○○○○○○○○○○○○○

DATE:	WEEK:	WEIGHT:

Warm Up/ Stretching		Duration:				

Exercise		Set 1	Set 2	Set 3	Set 4	Set 5
	Weight					
	Reps					
	Weight					
	Reps					
	Weight					
	Reps					
	Weight					
	Reps					
	Weight					
	Reps					
	Weight					
	Reps					
	Weight					
	Reps					
	Weight					
	Reps					
	Weight					
	Reps					
	Weight					
	Reps					
	Weight					
	Reps					
	Weight					
	Reps					

CARDIO WORKOUT

Exercise	Duration	Pace	Heart Rate	Calories

WATER   1 cup per circle
(1 cup = 8 ounces ~ 240ml)   ○○○○○○○○○○○○○○○○○○

DATE:	WEEK:	WEIGHT:

Warm Up/ Stretching		Duration:

Exercise		Set 1	Set 2	Set 3	Set 4	Set 5
	Weight					
	Reps					
	Weight					
	Reps					
	Weight					
	Reps					
	Weight					
	Reps					
	Weight					
	Reps					
	Weight					
	Reps					
	Weight					
	Reps					
	Weight					
	Reps					
	Weight					
	Reps					
	Weight					
	Reps					
	Weight					
	Reps					
	Weight					
	Reps					

CARDIO WORKOUT

Exercise	Duration	Pace	Heart Rate	Calories

WATER 1 cup per circle
(1 cup = 8 ounces ~ 240ml) ○○○○○○○○○○○○○○○○○

DATE:		WEEK:		WEIGHT:	

Warm Up/ Stretching			Duration:	

Exercise		Set 1	Set 2	Set 3	Set 4	Set 5
	Weight					
	Reps					
	Weight					
	Reps					
	Weight					
	Reps					
	Weight					
	Reps					
	Weight					
	Reps					
	Weight					
	Reps					
	Weight					
	Reps					
	Weight					
	Reps					
	Weight					
	Reps					
	Weight					
	Reps					
	Weight					
	Reps					
	Weight					
	Reps					

CARDIO WORKOUT

Exercise	Duration	Pace	Heart Rate	Calories

WATER   1 cup per circle
(1 cup = 8 ounces ~ 240ml)   ○○○○○○○○○○○○○○○○○○

DATE:		WEEK:		WEIGHT:	

Warm Up/ Stretching		Duration:	

Exercise		Set 1	Set 2	Set 3	Set 4	Set 5
	Weight					
	Reps					
	Weight					
	Reps					
	Weight					
	Reps					
	Weight					
	Reps					
	Weight					
	Reps					
	Weight					
	Reps					
	Weight					
	Reps					
	Weight					
	Reps					
	Weight					
	Reps					
	Weight					
	Reps					
	Weight					
	Reps					
	Weight					
	Reps					
	Weight					
	Reps					

CARDIO WORKOUT

Exercise	Duration	Pace	Heart Rate	Calories

WATER   1 cup per circle
(1 cup = 8 ounces ~ 240ml)   ○○○○○○○○○○○○○○○○

DATE:		WEEK:		WEIGHT:	

Warm Up/ Stretching				Duration:	

Exercise		Set 1	Set 2	Set 3	Set 4	Set 5
	Weight					
	Reps					
	Weight					
	Reps					
	Weight					
	Reps					
	Weight					
	Reps					
	Weight					
	Reps					
	Weight					
	Reps					
	Weight					
	Reps					
	Weight					
	Reps					
	Weight					
	Reps					
	Weight					
	Reps					
	Weight					
	Reps					
	Weight					
	Reps					

CARDIO WORKOUT

Exercise	Duration	Pace	Heart Rate	Calories

WATER 1 cup per circle
(1 cup = 8 ounces ~ 240ml)   ○○○○○○○○○○○○○○○○○○○

DATE:		WEEK:		WEIGHT:	

Warm Up/ Stretching	Duration:

Exercise		Set 1	Set 2	Set 3	Set 4	Set 5
	Weight					
	Reps					
	Weight					
	Reps					
	Weight					
	Reps					
	Weight					
	Reps					
	Weight					
	Reps					
	Weight					
	Reps					
	Weight					
	Reps					
	Weight					
	Reps					
	Weight					
	Reps					
	Weight					
	Reps					
	Weight					
	Reps					
	Weight					
	Reps					

CARDIO WORKOUT

Exercise	Duration	Pace	Heart Rate	Calories

WATER   1 cup per circle
(1 cup = 8 ounces ~ 240ml)   ○○○○○○○○○○○○○○○○

DATE:	WEEK:	WEIGHT:

Warm Up/ Stretching			Duration:			

Exercise		Set 1	Set 2	Set 3	Set 4	Set 5
	Weight					
	Reps					
	Weight					
	Reps					
	Weight					
	Reps					
	Weight					
	Reps					
	Weight					
	Reps					
	Weight					
	Reps					
	Weight					
	Reps					
	Weight					
	Reps					
	Weight					
	Reps					
	Weight					
	Reps					
	Weight					
	Reps					
	Weight					
	Reps					
	Weight					
	Reps					

CARDIO WORKOUT

Exercise	Duration	Pace	Heart Rate	Calories

WATER   1 cup per circle
(1 cup = 8 ounces ~ 240ml)   ○○○○○○○○○○○○○○○○○○○

DATE:		WEEK:		WEIGHT:	

Warm Up/ Stretching				Duration:	

Exercise		Set 1	Set 2	Set 3	Set 4	Set 5
	Weight					
	Reps					
	Weight					
	Reps					
	Weight					
	Reps					
	Weight					
	Reps					
	Weight					
	Reps					
	Weight					
	Reps					
	Weight					
	Reps					
	Weight					
	Reps					
	Weight					
	Reps					
	Weight					
	Reps					
	Weight					
	Reps					
	Weight					
	Reps					
	Weight					
	Reps					

CARDIO WORKOUT

Exercise	Duration	Pace	Heart Rate	Calories

WATER 1 cup per circle
(1 cup = 8 ounces ~ 240ml)   ○○○○○○○○○○○○○○○○○

DATE:	WEEK:	WEIGHT:

Warm Up/ Stretching						Duration:	

Exercise		Set 1	Set 2	Set 3	Set 4	Set 5
	Weight					
	Reps					
	Weight					
	Reps					
	Weight					
	Reps					
	Weight					
	Reps					
	Weight					
	Reps					
	Weight					
	Reps					
	Weight					
	Reps					
	Weight					
	Reps					
	Weight					
	Reps					
	Weight					
	Reps					
	Weight					
	Reps					
	Weight					
	Reps					

CARDIO WORKOUT

Exercise	Duration	Pace	Heart Rate	Calories

WATER   1 cup per circle
(1 cup = 8 ounces ~ 240ml)   ○○○○○○○○○○○○○○○○

DATE: **WEEK:** **WEIGHT:**

| Warm Up/ Stretching | | | | Duration: | |

Exercise		Set 1	Set 2	Set 3	Set 4	Set 5
	Weight					
	Reps					
	Weight					
	Reps					
	Weight					
	Reps					
	Weight					
	Reps					
	Weight					
	Reps					
	Weight					
	Reps					
	Weight					
	Reps					
	Weight					
	Reps					
	Weight					
	Reps					
	Weight					
	Reps					
	Weight					
	Reps					
	Weight					
	Reps					
	Weight					
	Reps					

CARDIO WORKOUT

Exercise	Duration	Pace	Heart Rate	Calories

WATER   1 cup per circle
(1 cup = 8 ounces ~ 240ml)   ○○○○○○○○○○○○○○○○○

DATE:	WEEK:	WEIGHT:

Warm Up/ Stretching	Duration:

Exercise		Set 1	Set 2	Set 3	Set 4	Set 5
	Weight					
	Reps					
	Weight					
	Reps					
	Weight					
	Reps					
	Weight					
	Reps					
	Weight					
	Reps					
	Weight					
	Reps					
	Weight					
	Reps					
	Weight					
	Reps					
	Weight					
	Reps					
	Weight					
	Reps					
	Weight					
	Reps					
	Weight					
	Reps					

CARDIO WORKOUT

Exercise	Duration	Pace	Heart Rate	Calories

WATER 1 cup per circle
(1 cup = 8 ounces ~ 240ml)   ○○○○○○○○○○○○○○○○○

DATE:	WEEK:	WEIGHT:

Warm Up/ Stretching	Duration:

Exercise		Set 1	Set 2	Set 3	Set 4	Set 5
	Weight					
	Reps					
	Weight					
	Reps					
	Weight					
	Reps					
	Weight					
	Reps					
	Weight					
	Reps					
	Weight					
	Reps					
	Weight					
	Reps					
	Weight					
	Reps					
	Weight					
	Reps					
	Weight					
	Reps					
	Weight					
	Reps					
	Weight					
	Reps					
	Weight					
	Reps					

CARDIO WORKOUT

Exercise	Duration	Pace	Heart Rate	Calories

WATER   1 cup per circle
(1 cup = 8 ounces ~ 240ml)   ○○○○○○○○○○○○○○○○○○

DATE: | **WEEK:** | **WEIGHT:**

Warm Up/ Stretching		Duration:

Exercise		Set 1	Set 2	Set 3	Set 4	Set 5
	Weight					
	Reps					
	Weight					
	Reps					
	Weight					
	Reps					
	Weight					
	Reps					
	Weight					
	Reps					
	Weight					
	Reps					
	Weight					
	Reps					
	Weight					
	Reps					
	Weight					
	Reps					
	Weight					
	Reps					
	Weight					
	Reps					
	Weight					
	Reps					

CARDIO WORKOUT

Exercise	Duration	Pace	Heart Rate	Calories

WATER   1 cup per circle
(1 cup = 8 ounces ~ 240ml)   ○○○○○○○○○○○○○○○○○○○

DATE:		WEEK:		WEIGHT:	

Warm Up/ Stretching		Duration:	

Exercise		Set 1	Set 2	Set 3	Set 4	Set 5
	Weight					
	Reps					
	Weight					
	Reps					
	Weight					
	Reps					
	Weight					
	Reps					
	Weight					
	Reps					
	Weight					
	Reps					
	Weight					
	Reps					
	Weight					
	Reps					
	Weight					
	Reps					
	Weight					
	Reps					
	Weight					
	Reps					
	Weight					
	Reps					

CARDIO WORKOUT

Exercise	Duration	Pace	Heart Rate	Calories

WATER 1 cup per circle
(1 cup = 8 ounces ~ 240ml)   ○○○○○○○○○○○○○○○○

DATE:	WEEK:	WEIGHT:

Warm Up/ Stretching		Duration:

Exercise		Set 1	Set 2	Set 3	Set 4	Set 5
	Weight					
	Reps					
	Weight					
	Reps					
	Weight					
	Reps					
	Weight					
	Reps					
	Weight					
	Reps					
	Weight					
	Reps					
	Weight					
	Reps					
	Weight					
	Reps					
	Weight					
	Reps					
	Weight					
	Reps					
	Weight					
	Reps					
	Weight					
	Reps					

CARDIO WORKOUT

Exercise	Duration	Pace	Heart Rate	Calories

WATER   1 cup per circle
(1 cup = 8 ounces ~ 240ml)   ○○○○○○○○○○○○○○○○

DATE:	WEEK:	WEIGHT:

Warm Up/ Stretching	Duration:

Exercise		Set 1	Set 2	Set 3	Set 4	Set 5
	Weight					
	Reps					
	Weight					
	Reps					
	Weight					
	Reps					
	Weight					
	Reps					
	Weight					
	Reps					
	Weight					
	Reps					
	Weight					
	Reps					
	Weight					
	Reps					
	Weight					
	Reps					
	Weight					
	Reps					
	Weight					
	Reps					
	Weight					
	Reps					
	Weight					
	Reps					

CARDIO WORKOUT

Exercise	Duration	Pace	Heart Rate	Calories

WATER   1 cup per circle
(1 cup = 8 ounces ~ 240ml)   ○○○○○○○○○○○○○○○○○○○

DATE:	WEEK:	WEIGHT:

Warm Up/ Stretching	Duration:

Exercise		Set 1	Set 2	Set 3	Set 4	Set 5
	Weight					
	Reps					
	Weight					
	Reps					
	Weight					
	Reps					
	Weight					
	Reps					
	Weight					
	Reps					
	Weight					
	Reps					
	Weight					
	Reps					
	Weight					
	Reps					
	Weight					
	Reps					
	Weight					
	Reps					
	Weight					
	Reps					
	Weight					
	Reps					

CARDIO WORKOUT

Exercise	Duration	Pace	Heart Rate	Calories

WATER   1 cup per circle
(1 cup = 8 ounces ~ 240ml)   ○○○○○○○○○○○○○○○○○

DATE:	WEEK:	WEIGHT:

Warm Up/ Stretching	Duration:

Exercise		Set 1	Set 2	Set 3	Set 4	Set 5
	Weight					
	Reps					
	Weight					
	Reps					
	Weight					
	Reps					
	Weight					
	Reps					
	Weight					
	Reps					
	Weight					
	Reps					
	Weight					
	Reps					
	Weight					
	Reps					
	Weight					
	Reps					
	Weight					
	Reps					
	Weight					
	Reps					
	Weight					
	Reps					

CARDIO WORKOUT

Exercise	Duration	Pace	Heart Rate	Calories

WATER   1 cup per circle
(1 cup = 8 ounces ~ 240ml)   ○○○○○○○○○○○○○○○○○

DATE: _____ **WEEK:** _____ **WEIGHT:** _____

Warm Up/ Stretching		Duration:

Exercise		Set 1	Set 2	Set 3	Set 4	Set 5
	Weight					
	Reps					
	Weight					
	Reps					
	Weight					
	Reps					
	Weight					
	Reps					
	Weight					
	Reps					
	Weight					
	Reps					
	Weight					
	Reps					
	Weight					
	Reps					
	Weight					
	Reps					
	Weight					
	Reps					
	Weight					
	Reps					
	Weight					
	Reps					

CARDIO WORKOUT

Exercise	Duration	Pace	Heart Rate	Calories

WATER   1 cup per circle
(1 cup = 8 ounces ~ 240ml)   ○○○○○○○○○○○○○○○○○

DATE:		WEEK:		WEIGHT:	

Warm Up/ Stretching				Duration:	

Exercise		Set 1	Set 2	Set 3	Set 4	Set 5
	Weight					
	Reps					
	Weight					
	Reps					
	Weight					
	Reps					
	Weight					
	Reps					
	Weight					
	Reps					
	Weight					
	Reps					
	Weight					
	Reps					
	Weight					
	Reps					
	Weight					
	Reps					
	Weight					
	Reps					
	Weight					
	Reps					
	Weight					
	Reps					

CARDIO WORKOUT

Exercise	Duration	Pace	Heart Rate	Calories

WATER   1 cup per circle
(1 cup = 8 ounces ~ 240ml)   ○○○○○○○○○○○○○○○○○

DATE:	WEEK:	WEIGHT:

Warm Up/ Stretching		Duration:

Exercise		Set 1	Set 2	Set 3	Set 4	Set 5
	Weight					
	Reps					
	Weight					
	Reps					
	Weight					
	Reps					
	Weight					
	Reps					
	Weight					
	Reps					
	Weight					
	Reps					
	Weight					
	Reps					
	Weight					
	Reps					
	Weight					
	Reps					
	Weight					
	Reps					
	Weight					
	Reps					
	Weight					
	Reps					

CARDIO WORKOUT

Exercise	Duration	Pace	Heart Rate	Calories

WATER   1 cup per circle
(1 cup = 8 ounces ~ 240ml)   ○○○○○○○○○○○○○○○○

DATE:	WEEK:	WEIGHT:

Warm Up/ Stretching	Duration:

Exercise		Set 1	Set 2	Set 3	Set 4	Set 5
	Weight					
	Reps					
	Weight					
	Reps					
	Weight					
	Reps					
	Weight					
	Reps					
	Weight					
	Reps					
	Weight					
	Reps					
	Weight					
	Reps					
	Weight					
	Reps					
	Weight					
	Reps					
	Weight					
	Reps					
	Weight					
	Reps					
	Weight					
	Reps					

CARDIO WORKOUT

Exercise	Duration	Pace	Heart Rate	Calories

WATER   1 cup per circle
(1 cup = 8 ounces ~ 240ml)   ○○○○○○○○○○○○○○○○

DATE: **WEEK:**   **WEIGHT:**

Warm Up/ Stretching						**Duration:**

Exercise		Set 1	Set 2	Set 3	Set 4	Set 5
	Weight					
	Reps					
	Weight					
	Reps					
	Weight					
	Reps					
	Weight					
	Reps					
	Weight					
	Reps					
	Weight					
	Reps					
	Weight					
	Reps					
	Weight					
	Reps					
	Weight					
	Reps					
	Weight					
	Reps					
	Weight					
	Reps					
	Weight					
	Reps					
	Weight					
	Reps					

CARDIO WORKOUT

Exercise	Duration	Pace	Heart Rate	Calories

WATER   1 cup per circle
(1 cup = 8 ounces ~ 240ml)   ○○○○○○○○○○○○○○○○○○

DATE:		WEEK:		WEIGHT:	

Warm Up/ Stretching	Duration:

Exercise		Set 1	Set 2	Set 3	Set 4	Set 5
	Weight					
	Reps					
	Weight					
	Reps					
	Weight					
	Reps					
	Weight					
	Reps					
	Weight					
	Reps					
	Weight					
	Reps					
	Weight					
	Reps					
	Weight					
	Reps					
	Weight					
	Reps					
	Weight					
	Reps					
	Weight					
	Reps					
	Weight					
	Reps					

CARDIO WORKOUT

Exercise	Duration	Pace	Heart Rate	Calories

WATER   1 cup per circle
(1 cup = 8 ounces ~ 240ml)   ○○○○○○○○○○○○○○○○

DATE: _____ **WEEK:** _____ **WEIGHT:** _____

Warm Up/ Stretching					Duration:	

Exercise		Set 1	Set 2	Set 3	Set 4	Set 5
	Weight					
	Reps					
	Weight					
	Reps					
	Weight					
	Reps					
	Weight					
	Reps					
	Weight					
	Reps					
	Weight					
	Reps					
	Weight					
	Reps					
	Weight					
	Reps					
	Weight					
	Reps					
	Weight					
	Reps					
	Weight					
	Reps					
	Weight					
	Reps					
	Weight					
	Reps					

CARDIO WORKOUT

Exercise	Duration	Pace	Heart Rate	Calories

WATER   1 cup per circle
(1 cup = 8 ounces ~ 240ml)   ○○○○○○○○○○○○○○○○○

DATE:		WEEK:		WEIGHT:	

Warm Up/ Stretching   Duration:

Exercise		Set 1	Set 2	Set 3	Set 4	Set 5
	Weight					
	Reps					
	Weight					
	Reps					
	Weight					
	Reps					
	Weight					
	Reps					
	Weight					
	Reps					
	Weight					
	Reps					
	Weight					
	Reps					
	Weight					
	Reps					
	Weight					
	Reps					
	Weight					
	Reps					
	Weight					
	Reps					
	Weight					
	Reps					

CARDIO WORKOUT

Exercise	Duration	Pace	Heart Rate	Calories

WATER   1 cup per circle
(1 cup = 8 ounces ~ 240ml)   ○○○○○○○○○○○○○○○○○○

DATE: _____ **WEEK:** _____ **WEIGHT:** _____

Warm Up/ Stretching		Duration:	

Exercise		Set 1	Set 2	Set 3	Set 4	Set 5
	Weight					
	Reps					
	Weight					
	Reps					
	Weight					
	Reps					
	Weight					
	Reps					
	Weight					
	Reps					
	Weight					
	Reps					
	Weight					
	Reps					
	Weight					
	Reps					
	Weight					
	Reps					
	Weight					
	Reps					
	Weight					
	Reps					
	Weight					
	Reps					
	Weight					
	Reps					
	Weight					
	Reps					

CARDIO WORKOUT

Exercise	Duration	Pace	Heart Rate	Calories

WATER 1 cup per circle
(1 cup = 8 ounces ~ 240ml)   ○○○○○○○○○○○○○○○○○○○○

DATE: **WEEK:**   **WEIGHT:**

| Warm Up/ Stretching | | | | | | Duration: | |

Exercise		Set 1	Set 2	Set 3	Set 4	Set 5
	Weight					
	Reps					
	Weight					
	Reps					
	Weight					
	Reps					
	Weight					
	Reps					
	Weight					
	Reps					
	Weight					
	Reps					
	Weight					
	Reps					
	Weight					
	Reps					
	Weight					
	Reps					
	Weight					
	Reps					
	Weight					
	Reps					
	Weight					
	Reps					

CARDIO WORKOUT

Exercise	Duration	Pace	Heart Rate	Calories

WATER   1 cup per circle
(1 cup = 8 ounces ~ 240ml)   ○○○○○○○○○○○○○○○○○

DATE:	WEEK:	WEIGHT:

Warm Up/ Stretching		Duration:

Exercise		Set 1	Set 2	Set 3	Set 4	Set 5
	Weight					
	Reps					
	Weight					
	Reps					
	Weight					
	Reps					
	Weight					
	Reps					
	Weight					
	Reps					
	Weight					
	Reps					
	Weight					
	Reps					
	Weight					
	Reps					
	Weight					
	Reps					
	Weight					
	Reps					
	Weight					
	Reps					
	Weight					
	Reps					
	Weight					
	Reps					

CARDIO WORKOUT

Exercise	Duration	Pace	Heart Rate	Calories

WATER   1 cup per circle
(1 cup = 8 ounces ~ 240ml)   ○○○○○○○○○○○○○○○○○○○

DATE:	WEEK:	WEIGHT:

Warm Up/ Stretching	Duration:

Exercise		Set 1	Set 2	Set 3	Set 4	Set 5
	Weight					
	Reps					
	Weight					
	Reps					
	Weight					
	Reps					
	Weight					
	Reps					
	Weight					
	Reps					
	Weight					
	Reps					
	Weight					
	Reps					
	Weight					
	Reps					
	Weight					
	Reps					
	Weight					
	Reps					
	Weight					
	Reps					
	Weight					
	Reps					
	Weight					
	Reps					

CARDIO WORKOUT

Exercise	Duration	Pace	Heart Rate	Calories

WATER 1 cup per circle
(1 cup = 8 ounces ~ 240ml)   ○○○○○○○○○○○○○○○○

DATE:		WEEK:		WEIGHT:	

Warm Up/ Stretching			Duration:	

Exercise		Set 1	Set 2	Set 3	Set 4	Set 5
	Weight					
	Reps					
	Weight					
	Reps					
	Weight					
	Reps					
	Weight					
	Reps					
	Weight					
	Reps					
	Weight					
	Reps					
	Weight					
	Reps					
	Weight					
	Reps					
	Weight					
	Reps					
	Weight					
	Reps					
	Weight					
	Reps					
	Weight					
	Reps					

CARDIO WORKOUT

Exercise	Duration	Pace	Heart Rate	Calories

WATER   1 cup per circle
(1 cup = 8 ounces ~ 240ml)   ○○○○○○○○○○○○○○○○○○

DATE: | **WEEK:** | **WEIGHT:**

Warm Up/ Stretching		Duration:	

Exercise		Set 1	Set 2	Set 3	Set 4	Set 5
	Weight					
	Reps					
	Weight					
	Reps					
	Weight					
	Reps					
	Weight					
	Reps					
	Weight					
	Reps					
	Weight					
	Reps					
	Weight					
	Reps					
	Weight					
	Reps					
	Weight					
	Reps					
	Weight					
	Reps					
	Weight					
	Reps					
	Weight					
	Reps					

CARDIO WORKOUT

Exercise	Duration	Pace	Heart Rate	Calories

WATER   1 cup per circle
(1 cup = 8 ounces ~ 240ml)   ○○○○○○○○○○○○○○○

DATE: _____ **WEEK:** _____ **WEIGHT:** _____

Warm Up/ Stretching					Duration:	_____

Exercise		Set 1	Set 2	Set 3	Set 4	Set 5
	Weight					
	Reps					
	Weight					
	Reps					
	Weight					
	Reps					
	Weight					
	Reps					
	Weight					
	Reps					
	Weight					
	Reps					
	Weight					
	Reps					
	Weight					
	Reps					
	Weight					
	Reps					
	Weight					
	Reps					
	Weight					
	Reps					
	Weight					
	Reps					

CARDIO WORKOUT

Exercise	Duration	Pace	Heart Rate	Calories

WATER   1 cup per circle
(1 cup = 8 ounces ~ 240ml)   ○○○○○○○○○○○○○○○○○○

DATE:	WEEK:	WEIGHT:

Warm Up/ Stretching	Duration:

Exercise		Set 1	Set 2	Set 3	Set 4	Set 5
	Weight					
	Reps					
	Weight					
	Reps					
	Weight					
	Reps					
	Weight					
	Reps					
	Weight					
	Reps					
	Weight					
	Reps					
	Weight					
	Reps					
	Weight					
	Reps					
	Weight					
	Reps					
	Weight					
	Reps					
	Weight					
	Reps					
	Weight					
	Reps					

CARDIO WORKOUT

Exercise	Duration	Pace	Heart Rate	Calories

WATER   1 cup per circle
(1 cup = 8 ounces ~ 240ml)   ○○○○○○○○○○○○○○○○○

DATE: _____ **WEEK:** ____ **WEIGHT:** _____

Warm Up/ Stretching						**Duration:**	

Exercise		Set 1	Set 2	Set 3	Set 4	Set 5
	Weight					
	Reps					
	Weight					
	Reps					
	Weight					
	Reps					
	Weight					
	Reps					
	Weight					
	Reps					
	Weight					
	Reps					
	Weight					
	Reps					
	Weight					
	Reps					
	Weight					
	Reps					
	Weight					
	Reps					
	Weight					
	Reps					
	Weight					
	Reps					

CARDIO WORKOUT

Exercise	Duration	Pace	Heart Rate	Calories

WATER 1 cup per circle
(1 cup = 8 ounces ~ 240ml)   ○○○○○○○○○○○○○○○○

DATE:		WEEK:		WEIGHT:	

Warm Up/ Stretching				Duration:	

Exercise		Set 1	Set 2	Set 3	Set 4	Set 5
	Weight					
	Reps					
	Weight					
	Reps					
	Weight					
	Reps					
	Weight					
	Reps					
	Weight					
	Reps					
	Weight					
	Reps					
	Weight					
	Reps					
	Weight					
	Reps					
	Weight					
	Reps					
	Weight					
	Reps					
	Weight					
	Reps					
	Weight					
	Reps					
	Weight					
	Reps					

CARDIO WORKOUT

Exercise	Duration	Pace	Heart Rate	Calories

WATER 1 cup per circle
(1 cup = 8 ounces ~ 240ml)   ○○○○○○○○○○○○○○○

DATE:	WEEK:	WEIGHT:

Warm Up/ Stretching	Duration:

Exercise		Set 1	Set 2	Set 3	Set 4	Set 5
	Weight					
	Reps					
	Weight					
	Reps					
	Weight					
	Reps					
	Weight					
	Reps					
	Weight					
	Reps					
	Weight					
	Reps					
	Weight					
	Reps					
	Weight					
	Reps					
	Weight					
	Reps					
	Weight					
	Reps					
	Weight					
	Reps					
	Weight					
	Reps					

CARDIO WORKOUT

Exercise	Duration	Pace	Heart Rate	Calories

WATER   1 cup per circle
(1 cup = 8 ounces ~ 240ml)   ○○○○○○○○○○○○○○○○

DATE:		WEEK:		WEIGHT:	

Warm Up/ Stretching   **Duration:**

Exercise		Set 1	Set 2	Set 3	Set 4	Set 5
	Weight					
	Reps					
	Weight					
	Reps					
	Weight					
	Reps					
	Weight					
	Reps					
	Weight					
	Reps					
	Weight					
	Reps					
	Weight					
	Reps					
	Weight					
	Reps					
	Weight					
	Reps					
	Weight					
	Reps					
	Weight					
	Reps					
	Weight					
	Reps					

CARDIO WORKOUT

Exercise	Duration	Pace	Heart Rate	Calories

WATER   1 cup per circle
(1 cup = 8 ounces ~ 240ml)   ○○○○○○○○○○○○○○○○

DATE:		WEEK:		WEIGHT:	

Warm Up/ Stretching				Duration:	

Exercise		Set 1	Set 2	Set 3	Set 4	Set 5
	Weight					
	Reps					
	Weight					
	Reps					
	Weight					
	Reps					
	Weight					
	Reps					
	Weight					
	Reps					
	Weight					
	Reps					
	Weight					
	Reps					
	Weight					
	Reps					
	Weight					
	Reps					
	Weight					
	Reps					
	Weight					
	Reps					
	Weight					
	Reps					
	Weight					
	Reps					

CARDIO WORKOUT

Exercise	Duration	Pace	Heart Rate	Calories

WATER   1 cup per circle
(1 cup = 8 ounces ~ 240ml)   ○○○○○○○○○○○○○○○○○○

DATE:		WEEK:		WEIGHT:	

Warm Up/ Stretching   **Duration:** [   ]

Exercise		Set 1	Set 2	Set 3	Set 4	Set 5
	Weight					
	Reps					
	Weight					
	Reps					
	Weight					
	Reps					
	Weight					
	Reps					
	Weight					
	Reps					
	Weight					
	Reps					
	Weight					
	Reps					
	Weight					
	Reps					
	Weight					
	Reps					
	Weight					
	Reps					
	Weight					
	Reps					
	Weight					
	Reps					

CARDIO WORKOUT

Exercise	Duration	Pace	Heart Rate	Calories

WATER   1 cup per circle
(1 cup = 8 ounces ~ 240ml)   ◯◯◯◯◯◯◯◯◯◯◯◯◯◯◯◯

DATE:		WEEK:		WEIGHT:	

Warm Up/ Stretching		Duration:	

Exercise		Set 1	Set 2	Set 3	Set 4	Set 5
	Weight					
	Reps					
	Weight					
	Reps					
	Weight					
	Reps					
	Weight					
	Reps					
	Weight					
	Reps					
	Weight					
	Reps					
	Weight					
	Reps					
	Weight					
	Reps					
	Weight					
	Reps					
	Weight					
	Reps					
	Weight					
	Reps					
	Weight					
	Reps					

CARDIO WORKOUT

Exercise	Duration	Pace	Heart Rate	Calories

WATER   1 cup per circle
(1 cup = 8 ounces ~ 240ml)   ○○○○○○○○○○○○○○○○○

DATE: | **WEEK:** | **WEIGHT:**

Warm Up/ Stretching   **Duration:**

Exercise		Set 1	Set 2	Set 3	Set 4	Set 5
	Weight					
	Reps					
	Weight					
	Reps					
	Weight					
	Reps					
	Weight					
	Reps					
	Weight					
	Reps					
	Weight					
	Reps					
	Weight					
	Reps					
	Weight					
	Reps					
	Weight					
	Reps					
	Weight					
	Reps					
	Weight					
	Reps					
	Weight					
	Reps					
	Weight					
	Reps					

CARDIO WORKOUT

Exercise	Duration	Pace	Heart Rate	Calories

WATER   1 cup per circle
(1 cup = 8 ounces ~ 240ml)   ◯ ◯ ◯ ◯ ◯ ◯ ◯ ◯ ◯ ◯ ◯ ◯ ◯ ◯ ◯ ◯ ◯

DATE:		WEEK:		WEIGHT:	

Warm Up/ Stretching   Duration: [ ]

Exercise		Set 1	Set 2	Set 3	Set 4	Set 5
	Weight					
	Reps					
	Weight					
	Reps					
	Weight					
	Reps					
	Weight					
	Reps					
	Weight					
	Reps					
	Weight					
	Reps					
	Weight					
	Reps					
	Weight					
	Reps					
	Weight					
	Reps					
	Weight					
	Reps					
	Weight					
	Reps					
	Weight					
	Reps					
	Weight					
	Reps					

CARDIO WORKOUT

Exercise	Duration	Pace	Heart Rate	Calories

WATER   1 cup per circle
(1 cup = 8 ounces ~ 240ml)   ○○○○○○○○○○○○○○○○

DATE:	WEEK:	WEIGHT:

Warm Up/ Stretching Duration:

Exercise		Set 1	Set 2	Set 3	Set 4	Set 5
	Weight					
	Reps					
	Weight					
	Reps					
	Weight					
	Reps					
	Weight					
	Reps					
	Weight					
	Reps					
	Weight					
	Reps					
	Weight					
	Reps					
	Weight					
	Reps					
	Weight					
	Reps					
	Weight					
	Reps					
	Weight					
	Reps					
	Weight					
	Reps					

CARDIO WORKOUT

Exercise	Duration	Pace	Heart Rate	Calories

WATER   1 cup per circle
(1 cup = 8 ounces ~ 240ml)   ◯ ◯ ◯ ◯ ◯ ◯ ◯ ◯ ◯ ◯ ◯ ◯ ◯ ◯ ◯ ◯

DATE:		WEEK:		WEIGHT:	

Warm Up/ Stretching   **Duration:**

Exercise		Set 1	Set 2	Set 3	Set 4	Set 5
	Weight					
	Reps					
	Weight					
	Reps					
	Weight					
	Reps					
	Weight					
	Reps					
	Weight					
	Reps					
	Weight					
	Reps					
	Weight					
	Reps					
	Weight					
	Reps					
	Weight					
	Reps					
	Weight					
	Reps					
	Weight					
	Reps					
	Weight					
	Reps					

CARDIO WORKOUT

Exercise	Duration	Pace	Heart Rate	Calories

WATER   1 cup per circle
(1 cup = 8 ounces ~ 240ml)   ○○○○○○○○○○○○○○○○○

DATE:		WEEK:		WEIGHT:	

Warm Up/ Stretching Duration:

Exercise		Set 1	Set 2	Set 3	Set 4	Set 5
	Weight					
	Reps					
	Weight					
	Reps					
	Weight					
	Reps					
	Weight					
	Reps					
	Weight					
	Reps					
	Weight					
	Reps					
	Weight					
	Reps					
	Weight					
	Reps					
	Weight					
	Reps					
	Weight					
	Reps					
	Weight					
	Reps					
	Weight					
	Reps					

CARDIO WORKOUT

Exercise	Duration	Pace	Heart Rate	Calories

WATER   1 cup per circle
(1 cup = 8 ounces ~ 240ml)   ○○○○○○○○○○○○○○○○○○

DATE:		WEEK:		WEIGHT:	

Warm Up/ Stretching					Duration:	

Exercise		Set 1	Set 2	Set 3	Set 4	Set 5
	Weight					
	Reps					
	Weight					
	Reps					
	Weight					
	Reps					
	Weight					
	Reps					
	Weight					
	Reps					
	Weight					
	Reps					
	Weight					
	Reps					
	Weight					
	Reps					
	Weight					
	Reps					
	Weight					
	Reps					
	Weight					
	Reps					
	Weight					
	Reps					
	Weight					
	Reps					

CARDIO WORKOUT

Exercise	Duration	Pace	Heart Rate	Calories

WATER   1 cup per circle
(1 cup = 8 ounces ~ 240ml)   ○○○○○○○○○○○○○○○○○○

DATE:		WEEK:		WEIGHT:	

Warm Up/ Stretching   Duration:

Exercise		Set 1	Set 2	Set 3	Set 4	Set 5
	Weight					
	Reps					
	Weight					
	Reps					
	Weight					
	Reps					
	Weight					
	Reps					
	Weight					
	Reps					
	Weight					
	Reps					
	Weight					
	Reps					
	Weight					
	Reps					
	Weight					
	Reps					
	Weight					
	Reps					
	Weight					
	Reps					
	Weight					
	Reps					
	Weight					
	Reps					

CARDIO WORKOUT

Exercise	Duration	Pace	Heart Rate	Calories

WATER   1 cup per circle
(1 cup = 8 ounces ~ 240ml)   ○○○○○○○○○○○○○○○○○○

DATE:		WEEK:		WEIGHT:	

Warm Up/ Stretching	Duration:

Exercise		Set 1	Set 2	Set 3	Set 4	Set 5
	Weight					
	Reps					
	Weight					
	Reps					
	Weight					
	Reps					
	Weight					
	Reps					
	Weight					
	Reps					
	Weight					
	Reps					
	Weight					
	Reps					
	Weight					
	Reps					
	Weight					
	Reps					
	Weight					
	Reps					
	Weight					
	Reps					
	Weight					
	Reps					

CARDIO WORKOUT

Exercise	Duration	Pace	Heart Rate	Calories

WATER   1 cup per circle
(1 cup = 8 ounces ~ 240ml)   ○○○○○○○○○○○○○○○○

DATE:	WEEK:	WEIGHT:

Warm Up/ Stretching Duration:

Exercise		Set 1	Set 2	Set 3	Set 4	Set 5
	Weight					
	Reps					
	Weight					
	Reps					
	Weight					
	Reps					
	Weight					
	Reps					
	Weight					
	Reps					
	Weight					
	Reps					
	Weight					
	Reps					
	Weight					
	Reps					
	Weight					
	Reps					
	Weight					
	Reps					
	Weight					
	Reps					
	Weight					
	Reps					

CARDIO WORKOUT

Exercise	Duration	Pace	Heart Rate	Calories

WATER   1 cup per circle
(1 cup = 8 ounces ~ 240ml)   ○ ○ ○ ○ ○ ○ ○ ○ ○ ○ ○ ○ ○ ○ ○ ○

DATE: **WEEK:**   **WEIGHT:**

Warm Up/ Stretching						Duration:

Exercise		Set 1	Set 2	Set 3	Set 4	Set 5
	Weight					
	Reps					
	Weight					
	Reps					
	Weight					
	Reps					
	Weight					
	Reps					
	Weight					
	Reps					
	Weight					
	Reps					
	Weight					
	Reps					
	Weight					
	Reps					
	Weight					
	Reps					
	Weight					
	Reps					
	Weight					
	Reps					
	Weight					
	Reps					
	Weight					
	Reps					

CARDIO WORKOUT

Exercise	Duration	Pace	Heart Rate	Calories

WATER   1 cup per circle
(1 cup = 8 ounces ~ 240ml)   ○○○○○○○○○○○○○○○○○

DATE:		WEEK:		WEIGHT:	

Warm Up/ Stretching **Duration:**

Exercise		Set 1	Set 2	Set 3	Set 4	Set 5
	Weight					
	Reps					
	Weight					
	Reps					
	Weight					
	Reps					
	Weight					
	Reps					
	Weight					
	Reps					
	Weight					
	Reps					
	Weight					
	Reps					
	Weight					
	Reps					
	Weight					
	Reps					
	Weight					
	Reps					
	Weight					
	Reps					
	Weight					
	Reps					

CARDIO WORKOUT

Exercise	Duration	Pace	Heart Rate	Calories

WATER   1 cup per circle
(1 cup = 8 ounces ~ 240ml)   ○ ○ ○ ○ ○ ○ ○ ○ ○ ○ ○ ○ ○ ○ ○ ○

DATE:	WEEK:	WEIGHT:

Warm Up/ Stretching				Duration:	

Exercise		Set 1	Set 2	Set 3	Set 4	Set 5
	Weight					
	Reps					
	Weight					
	Reps					
	Weight					
	Reps					
	Weight					
	Reps					
	Weight					
	Reps					
	Weight					
	Reps					
	Weight					
	Reps					
	Weight					
	Reps					
	Weight					
	Reps					
	Weight					
	Reps					
	Weight					
	Reps					
	Weight					
	Reps					

CARDIO WORKOUT

Exercise	Duration	Pace	Heart Rate	Calories

WATER 1 cup per circle
(1 cup = 8 ounces ~ 240ml)   ○○○○○○○○○○○○○○○○○

DATE:		WEEK:		WEIGHT:	

Warm Up/ Stretching Duration:

Exercise		Set 1	Set 2	Set 3	Set 4	Set 5
	Weight					
	Reps					
	Weight					
	Reps					
	Weight					
	Reps					
	Weight					
	Reps					
	Weight					
	Reps					
	Weight					
	Reps					
	Weight					
	Reps					
	Weight					
	Reps					
	Weight					
	Reps					
	Weight					
	Reps					
	Weight					
	Reps					
	Weight					
	Reps					

CARDIO WORKOUT

Exercise	Duration	Pace	Heart Rate	Calories

WATER   1 cup per circle
(1 cup = 8 ounces ~ 240ml)   ○ ○ ○ ○ ○ ○ ○ ○ ○ ○ ○ ○ ○ ○ ○ ○

DATE:		WEEK:		WEIGHT:	

Warm Up/ Stretching	Duration:

Exercise		Set 1	Set 2	Set 3	Set 4	Set 5
	Weight					
	Reps					
	Weight					
	Reps					
	Weight					
	Reps					
	Weight					
	Reps					
	Weight					
	Reps					
	Weight					
	Reps					
	Weight					
	Reps					
	Weight					
	Reps					
	Weight					
	Reps					
	Weight					
	Reps					
	Weight					
	Reps					
	Weight					
	Reps					
	Weight					
	Reps					

CARDIO WORKOUT

Exercise	Duration	Pace	Heart Rate	Calories

WATER 1 cup per circle
(1 cup = 8 ounces ~ 240ml)   ○○○○○○○○○○○○○○○○○

DATE:		WEEK:		WEIGHT:	

Warm Up/ Stretching Duration:

Exercise		Set 1	Set 2	Set 3	Set 4	Set 5
	Weight					
	Reps					
	Weight					
	Reps					
	Weight					
	Reps					
	Weight					
	Reps					
	Weight					
	Reps					
	Weight					
	Reps					
	Weight					
	Reps					
	Weight					
	Reps					
	Weight					
	Reps					
	Weight					
	Reps					
	Weight					
	Reps					
	Weight					
	Reps					
	Weight					
	Reps					
	Weight					
	Reps					

CARDIO WORKOUT

Exercise	Duration	Pace	Heart Rate	Calories

WATER   1 cup per circle
(1 cup = 8 ounces ~ 240ml)   ○ ○ ○ ○ ○ ○ ○ ○ ○ ○ ○ ○ ○ ○ ○

DATE:		WEEK:		WEIGHT:	

Warm Up/ Stretching			Duration:	

Exercise		Set 1	Set 2	Set 3	Set 4	Set 5
	Weight					
	Reps					
	Weight					
	Reps					
	Weight					
	Reps					
	Weight					
	Reps					
	Weight					
	Reps					
	Weight					
	Reps					
	Weight					
	Reps					
	Weight					
	Reps					
	Weight					
	Reps					
	Weight					
	Reps					
	Weight					
	Reps					
	Weight					
	Reps					

CARDIO WORKOUT

Exercise	Duration	Pace	Heart Rate	Calories

WATER   1 cup per circle
(1 cup = 8 ounces ~ 240ml)   ○○○○○○○○○○○○○○○○

DATE: **WEEK:**   **WEIGHT:**

Warm Up/ Stretching   **Duration:**

Exercise		Set 1	Set 2	Set 3	Set 4	Set 5
	Weight					
	Reps					
	Weight					
	Reps					
	Weight					
	Reps					
	Weight					
	Reps					
	Weight					
	Reps					
	Weight					
	Reps					
	Weight					
	Reps					
	Weight					
	Reps					
	Weight					
	Reps					
	Weight					
	Reps					
	Weight					
	Reps					
	Weight					
	Reps					

CARDIO WORKOUT

Exercise	Duration	Pace	Heart Rate	Calories

WATER   1 cup per circle
(1 cup = 8 ounces ~ 240ml)   ◯◯◯◯◯◯◯◯◯◯◯◯◯◯◯◯

DATE:		WEEK:		WEIGHT:	

Warm Up/ Stretching   Duration:

Exercise		Set 1	Set 2	Set 3	Set 4	Set 5
	Weight					
	Reps					
	Weight					
	Reps					
	Weight					
	Reps					
	Weight					
	Reps					
	Weight					
	Reps					
	Weight					
	Reps					
	Weight					
	Reps					
	Weight					
	Reps					
	Weight					
	Reps					
	Weight					
	Reps					
	Weight					
	Reps					
	Weight					
	Reps					

CARDIO WORKOUT

Exercise	Duration	Pace	Heart Rate	Calories

WATER   1 cup per circle
(1 cup = 8 ounces ~ 240ml)   ○○○○○○○○○○○○○○○○

DATE: **WEEK:**   **WEIGHT:**

Warm Up/ Stretching   **Duration:**

Exercise		Set 1	Set 2	Set 3	Set 4	Set 5
	Weight					
	Reps					
	Weight					
	Reps					
	Weight					
	Reps					
	Weight					
	Reps					
	Weight					
	Reps					
	Weight					
	Reps					
	Weight					
	Reps					
	Weight					
	Reps					
	Weight					
	Reps					
	Weight					
	Reps					
	Weight					
	Reps					
	Weight					
	Reps					

CARDIO WORKOUT

Exercise	Duration	Pace	Heart Rate	Calories

WATER   1 cup per circle
(1 cup = 8 ounces ~ 240ml)   ○ ○ ○ ○ ○ ○ ○ ○ ○ ○ ○ ○ ○ ○ ○ ○ ○

DATE:		WEEK:		WEIGHT:	

Warm Up/ Stretching	Duration:

Exercise		Set 1	Set 2	Set 3	Set 4	Set 5
	Weight					
	Reps					
	Weight					
	Reps					
	Weight					
	Reps					
	Weight					
	Reps					
	Weight					
	Reps					
	Weight					
	Reps					
	Weight					
	Reps					
	Weight					
	Reps					
	Weight					
	Reps					
	Weight					
	Reps					
	Weight					
	Reps					
	Weight					
	Reps					

CARDIO WORKOUT

Exercise	Duration	Pace	Heart Rate	Calories

WATER   1 cup per circle
(1 cup = 8 ounces ~ 240ml)   ○○○○○○○○○○○○○○○

DATE:	WEEK:	WEIGHT:

Warm Up/ Stretching Duration:

Exercise		Set 1	Set 2	Set 3	Set 4	Set 5
	Weight					
	Reps					
	Weight					
	Reps					
	Weight					
	Reps					
	Weight					
	Reps					
	Weight					
	Reps					
	Weight					
	Reps					
	Weight					
	Reps					
	Weight					
	Reps					
	Weight					
	Reps					
	Weight					
	Reps					
	Weight					
	Reps					
	Weight					
	Reps					

CARDIO WORKOUT

Exercise	Duration	Pace	Heart Rate	Calories

WATER   1 cup per circle
(1 cup = 8 ounces ~ 240ml)   ○○○○○○○○○○○○○○○○○○

DATE:	WEEK:	WEIGHT:

Warm Up/ Stretching		Duration:

Exercise		Set 1	Set 2	Set 3	Set 4	Set 5
	Weight					
	Reps					
	Weight					
	Reps					
	Weight					
	Reps					
	Weight					
	Reps					
	Weight					
	Reps					
	Weight					
	Reps					
	Weight					
	Reps					
	Weight					
	Reps					
	Weight					
	Reps					
	Weight					
	Reps					
	Weight					
	Reps					
	Weight					
	Reps					
	Weight					
	Reps					

CARDIO WORKOUT

Exercise	Duration	Pace	Heart Rate	Calories

WATER   1 cup per circle
(1 cup = 8 ounces ~ 240ml)   ○ ○ ○ ○ ○ ○ ○ ○ ○ ○ ○ ○ ○ ○ ○

DATE:		WEEK:		WEIGHT:	

Warm Up/ Stretching   **Duration:**

Exercise		Set 1	Set 2	Set 3	Set 4	Set 5
	Weight					
	Reps					
	Weight					
	Reps					
	Weight					
	Reps					
	Weight					
	Reps					
	Weight					
	Reps					
	Weight					
	Reps					
	Weight					
	Reps					
	Weight					
	Reps					
	Weight					
	Reps					
	Weight					
	Reps					
	Weight					
	Reps					
	Weight					
	Reps					
	Weight					
	Reps					

CARDIO WORKOUT

Exercise	Duration	Pace	Heart Rate	Calories

WATER   1 cup per circle
(1 cup = 8 ounces ~ 240ml)   ○○○○○○○○○○○○○○○○○○

DATE:		WEEK:		WEIGHT:	

Warm Up/ Stretching				Duration:	

Exercise		Set 1	Set 2	Set 3	Set 4	Set 5
	Weight					
	Reps					
	Weight					
	Reps					
	Weight					
	Reps					
	Weight					
	Reps					
	Weight					
	Reps					
	Weight					
	Reps					
	Weight					
	Reps					
	Weight					
	Reps					
	Weight					
	Reps					
	Weight					
	Reps					
	Weight					
	Reps					
	Weight					
	Reps					

CARDIO WORKOUT

Exercise	Duration	Pace	Heart Rate	Calories

WATER 1 cup per circle
(1 cup = 8 ounces ~ 240ml)   ○○○○○○○○○○○○○○○○

DATE:	WEEK:	WEIGHT:

Warm Up/ Stretching   Duration:

Exercise		Set 1	Set 2	Set 3	Set 4	Set 5
	Weight					
	Reps					
	Weight					
	Reps					
	Weight					
	Reps					
	Weight					
	Reps					
	Weight					
	Reps					
	Weight					
	Reps					
	Weight					
	Reps					
	Weight					
	Reps					
	Weight					
	Reps					
	Weight					
	Reps					
	Weight					
	Reps					
	Weight					
	Reps					

CARDIO WORKOUT

Exercise	Duration	Pace	Heart Rate	Calories

WATER   1 cup per circle
(1 cup = 8 ounces ~ 240ml)   ○ ○ ○ ○ ○ ○ ○ ○ ○ ○ ○ ○ ○ ○ ○ ○

DATE:	WEEK:	WEIGHT:

Warm Up/ Stretching		Duration:

Exercise		Set 1	Set 2	Set 3	Set 4	Set 5
	Weight					
	Reps					
	Weight					
	Reps					
	Weight					
	Reps					
	Weight					
	Reps					
	Weight					
	Reps					
	Weight					
	Reps					
	Weight					
	Reps					
	Weight					
	Reps					
	Weight					
	Reps					
	Weight					
	Reps					
	Weight					
	Reps					
	Weight					
	Reps					

CARDIO WORKOUT

Exercise	Duration	Pace	Heart Rate	Calories

WATER   1 cup per circle
(1 cup = 8 ounces ~ 240ml)   ○○○○○○○○○○○○○○○○○○

DATE:	WEEK:	WEIGHT:

Warm Up/ Stretching   Duration:

Exercise		Set 1	Set 2	Set 3	Set 4	Set 5
	Weight					
	Reps					
	Weight					
	Reps					
	Weight					
	Reps					
	Weight					
	Reps					
	Weight					
	Reps					
	Weight					
	Reps					
	Weight					
	Reps					
	Weight					
	Reps					
	Weight					
	Reps					
	Weight					
	Reps					
	Weight					
	Reps					
	Weight					
	Reps					
	Weight					
	Reps					

CARDIO WORKOUT

Exercise	Duration	Pace	Heart Rate	Calories

WATER   1 cup per circle
(1 cup = 8 ounces ~ 240ml)   ○○○○○○○○○○○○○○○○○○

DATE:		WEEK:		WEIGHT:	

Warm Up/ Stretching	Duration:

Exercise		Set 1	Set 2	Set 3	Set 4	Set 5
	Weight					
	Reps					
	Weight					
	Reps					
	Weight					
	Reps					
	Weight					
	Reps					
	Weight					
	Reps					
	Weight					
	Reps					
	Weight					
	Reps					
	Weight					
	Reps					
	Weight					
	Reps					
	Weight					
	Reps					
	Weight					
	Reps					
	Weight					
	Reps					
	Weight					
	Reps					

CARDIO WORKOUT

Exercise	Duration	Pace	Heart Rate	Calories

WATER   1 cup per circle
(1 cup = 8 ounces ~ 240ml)   ○○○○○○○○○○○○○○○○○

DATE:	WEEK:	WEIGHT:

Warm Up/ Stretching **Duration:**

Exercise		Set 1	Set 2	Set 3	Set 4	Set 5
	Weight					
	Reps					
	Weight					
	Reps					
	Weight					
	Reps					
	Weight					
	Reps					
	Weight					
	Reps					
	Weight					
	Reps					
	Weight					
	Reps					
	Weight					
	Reps					
	Weight					
	Reps					
	Weight					
	Reps					
	Weight					
	Reps					
	Weight					
	Reps					

CARDIO WORKOUT

Exercise	Duration	Pace	Heart Rate	Calories

WATER   1 cup per circle
(1 cup = 8 ounces ~ 240ml)   ○○○○○○○○○○○○○○○○○○

DATE:		WEEK:		WEIGHT:	

Warm Up/ Stretching		Duration:	

Exercise		Set 1	Set 2	Set 3	Set 4	Set 5
	Weight					
	Reps					
	Weight					
	Reps					
	Weight					
	Reps					
	Weight					
	Reps					
	Weight					
	Reps					
	Weight					
	Reps					
	Weight					
	Reps					
	Weight					
	Reps					
	Weight					
	Reps					
	Weight					
	Reps					
	Weight					
	Reps					
	Weight					
	Reps					
	Weight					
	Reps					

CARDIO WORKOUT

Exercise	Duration	Pace	Heart Rate	Calories

WATER   1 cup per circle
(1 cup = 8 ounces ~ 240ml)   ○○○○○○○○○○○○○○○○○○

DATE:	WEEK:	WEIGHT:

Warm Up/ Stretching	Duration:

Exercise		Set 1	Set 2	Set 3	Set 4	Set 5
	Weight					
	Reps					
	Weight					
	Reps					
	Weight					
	Reps					
	Weight					
	Reps					
	Weight					
	Reps					
	Weight					
	Reps					
	Weight					
	Reps					
	Weight					
	Reps					
	Weight					
	Reps					
	Weight					
	Reps					
	Weight					
	Reps					
	Weight					
	Reps					
	Weight					
	Reps					

CARDIO WORKOUT

Exercise	Duration	Pace	Heart Rate	Calories

WATER 1 cup per circle
(1 cup = 8 ounces ~ 240ml)   ○ ○ ○ ○ ○ ○ ○ ○ ○ ○ ○ ○ ○ ○ ○ ○

DATE:		WEEK:		WEIGHT:	

Warm Up/ Stretching	Duration:

Exercise		Set 1	Set 2	Set 3	Set 4	Set 5
	Weight					
	Reps					
	Weight					
	Reps					
	Weight					
	Reps					
	Weight					
	Reps					
	Weight					
	Reps					
	Weight					
	Reps					
	Weight					
	Reps					
	Weight					
	Reps					
	Weight					
	Reps					
	Weight					
	Reps					
	Weight					
	Reps					
	Weight					
	Reps					

CARDIO WORKOUT

Exercise	Duration	Pace	Heart Rate	Calories

WATER   1 cup per circle
(1 cup = 8 ounces ~ 240ml)   ○ ○ ○ ○ ○ ○ ○ ○ ○ ○ ○ ○ ○ ○ ○ ○

DATE:	WEEK:	WEIGHT:

Warm Up/ Stretching	Duration:

Exercise		Set 1	Set 2	Set 3	Set 4	Set 5
	Weight					
	Reps					
	Weight					
	Reps					
	Weight					
	Reps					
	Weight					
	Reps					
	Weight					
	Reps					
	Weight					
	Reps					
	Weight					
	Reps					
	Weight					
	Reps					
	Weight					
	Reps					
	Weight					
	Reps					
	Weight					
	Reps					
	Weight					
	Reps					

CARDIO WORKOUT

Exercise	Duration	Pace	Heart Rate	Calories

WATER   1 cup per circle
(1 cup = 8 ounces ~ 240ml)   ○○○○○○○○○○○○○○○○○

DATE:	WEEK:	WEIGHT:

Warm Up/ Stretching		Duration:

Exercise		Set 1	Set 2	Set 3	Set 4	Set 5
	Weight					
	Reps					
	Weight					
	Reps					
	Weight					
	Reps					
	Weight					
	Reps					
	Weight					
	Reps					
	Weight					
	Reps					
	Weight					
	Reps					
	Weight					
	Reps					
	Weight					
	Reps					
	Weight					
	Reps					
	Weight					
	Reps					
	Weight					
	Reps					

CARDIO WORKOUT

Exercise	Duration	Pace	Heart Rate	Calories

WATER 1 cup per circle
(1 cup = 8 ounces ~ 240ml)   ○○○○○○○○○○○○○○○○○

DATE:	WEEK:	WEIGHT:

Warm Up/ Stretching Duration:

Exercise		Set 1	Set 2	Set 3	Set 4	Set 5
	Weight					
	Reps					
	Weight					
	Reps					
	Weight					
	Reps					
	Weight					
	Reps					
	Weight					
	Reps					
	Weight					
	Reps					
	Weight					
	Reps					
	Weight					
	Reps					
	Weight					
	Reps					
	Weight					
	Reps					
	Weight					
	Reps					
	Weight					
	Reps					

CARDIO WORKOUT

Exercise	Duration	Pace	Heart Rate	Calories

WATER   1 cup per circle
(1 cup = 8 ounces ~ 240ml)   ○○○○○○○○○○○○○○○○○○

DATE:	WEEK:	WEIGHT:

Warm Up/ Stretching			Duration:		

Exercise		Set 1	Set 2	Set 3	Set 4	Set 5
	Weight					
	Reps					
	Weight					
	Reps					
	Weight					
	Reps					
	Weight					
	Reps					
	Weight					
	Reps					
	Weight					
	Reps					
	Weight					
	Reps					
	Weight					
	Reps					
	Weight					
	Reps					
	Weight					
	Reps					
	Weight					
	Reps					
	Weight					
	Reps					
	Weight					
	Reps					

CARDIO WORKOUT

Exercise	Duration	Pace	Heart Rate	Calories

WATER 1 cup per circle
(1 cup = 8 ounces ~ 240ml) ○○○○○○○○○○○○○○○○

DATE:	WEEK:	WEIGHT:

Warm Up/ Stretching	Duration:

Exercise		Set 1	Set 2	Set 3	Set 4	Set 5
	Weight					
	Reps					
	Weight					
	Reps					
	Weight					
	Reps					
	Weight					
	Reps					
	Weight					
	Reps					
	Weight					
	Reps					
	Weight					
	Reps					
	Weight					
	Reps					
	Weight					
	Reps					
	Weight					
	Reps					
	Weight					
	Reps					
	Weight					
	Reps					

CARDIO WORKOUT

Exercise	Duration	Pace	Heart Rate	Calories

WATER   1 cup per circle
(1 cup = 8 ounces ~ 240ml)   ○○○○○○○○○○○○○○○○○○

DATE:		WEEK:		WEIGHT:	

Warm Up/ Stretching	Duration:

Exercise		Set 1	Set 2	Set 3	Set 4	Set 5
	Weight					
	Reps					
	Weight					
	Reps					
	Weight					
	Reps					
	Weight					
	Reps					
	Weight					
	Reps					
	Weight					
	Reps					
	Weight					
	Reps					
	Weight					
	Reps					
	Weight					
	Reps					
	Weight					
	Reps					
	Weight					
	Reps					
	Weight					
	Reps					

CARDIO WORKOUT

Exercise	Duration	Pace	Heart Rate	Calories

WATER   1 cup per circle
(1 cup = 8 ounces ~ 240ml)   ○○○○○○○○○○○○○○○○○

DATE:	WEEK:	WEIGHT:

Warm Up/ Stretching   **Duration:**

Exercise		Set 1	Set 2	Set 3	Set 4	Set 5
	Weight					
	Reps					
	Weight					
	Reps					
	Weight					
	Reps					
	Weight					
	Reps					
	Weight					
	Reps					
	Weight					
	Reps					
	Weight					
	Reps					
	Weight					
	Reps					
	Weight					
	Reps					
	Weight					
	Reps					
	Weight					
	Reps					
	Weight					
	Reps					

CARDIO WORKOUT

Exercise	Duration	Pace	Heart Rate	Calories

WATER   1 cup per circle
(1 cup = 8 ounces ~ 240ml)   ○○○○○○○○○○○○○○○○○○○○

DATE:	WEEK:	WEIGHT:

Warm Up/ Stretching	Duration:

Exercise		Set 1	Set 2	Set 3	Set 4	Set 5
	Weight					
	Reps					
	Weight					
	Reps					
	Weight					
	Reps					
	Weight					
	Reps					
	Weight					
	Reps					
	Weight					
	Reps					
	Weight					
	Reps					
	Weight					
	Reps					
	Weight					
	Reps					
	Weight					
	Reps					
	Weight					
	Reps					
	Weight					
	Reps					
	Weight					
	Reps					

CARDIO WORKOUT

Exercise	Duration	Pace	Heart Rate	Calories

WATER   1 cup per circle
(1 cup = 8 ounces ~ 240ml)   ○○○○○○○○○○○○○○○○○○

DATE:	WEEK:	WEIGHT:

Warm Up/ Stretching	Duration:

Exercise		Set 1	Set 2	Set 3	Set 4	Set 5
	Weight					
	Reps					
	Weight					
	Reps					
	Weight					
	Reps					
	Weight					
	Reps					
	Weight					
	Reps					
	Weight					
	Reps					
	Weight					
	Reps					
	Weight					
	Reps					
	Weight					
	Reps					
	Weight					
	Reps					
	Weight					
	Reps					
	Weight					
	Reps					

CARDIO WORKOUT

Exercise	Duration	Pace	Heart Rate	Calories

WATER 1 cup per circle
(1 cup = 8 ounces ~ 240ml)   ○ ○ ○ ○ ○ ○ ○ ○ ○ ○ ○ ○ ○ ○ ○ ○

DATE:		WEEK:		WEIGHT:	

Warm Up/ Stretching					Duration:	

Exercise		Set 1	Set 2	Set 3	Set 4	Set 5
	Weight					
	Reps					
	Weight					
	Reps					
	Weight					
	Reps					
	Weight					
	Reps					
	Weight					
	Reps					
	Weight					
	Reps					
	Weight					
	Reps					
	Weight					
	Reps					
	Weight					
	Reps					
	Weight					
	Reps					
	Weight					
	Reps					
	Weight					
	Reps					
	Weight					
	Reps					

CARDIO WORKOUT

Exercise	Duration	Pace	Heart Rate	Calories

WATER   1 cup per circle
(1 cup = 8 ounces ~ 240ml)   ○○○○○○○○○○○○○○○○○○

DATE:		WEEK:		WEIGHT:	

Warm Up/ Stretching   Duration: [ ]

Exercise		Set 1	Set 2	Set 3	Set 4	Set 5
	Weight					
	Reps					
	Weight					
	Reps					
	Weight					
	Reps					
	Weight					
	Reps					
	Weight					
	Reps					
	Weight					
	Reps					
	Weight					
	Reps					
	Weight					
	Reps					
	Weight					
	Reps					
	Weight					
	Reps					
	Weight					
	Reps					
	Weight					
	Reps					

CARDIO WORKOUT

Exercise	Duration	Pace	Heart Rate	Calories

WATER   1 cup per circle
(1 cup = 8 ounces ~ 240ml)   ○○○○○○○○○○○○○○○○○

DATE:	WEEK:	WEIGHT:

Warm Up/ Stretching		Duration:	

Exercise		Set 1	Set 2	Set 3	Set 4	Set 5
	Weight					
	Reps					
	Weight					
	Reps					
	Weight					
	Reps					
	Weight					
	Reps					
	Weight					
	Reps					
	Weight					
	Reps					
	Weight					
	Reps					
	Weight					
	Reps					
	Weight					
	Reps					
	Weight					
	Reps					
	Weight					
	Reps					
	Weight					
	Reps					
	Weight					
	Reps					

CARDIO WORKOUT

Exercise	Duration	Pace	Heart Rate	Calories

WATER   1 cup per circle
(1 cup = 8 ounces ~ 240ml)   ○○○○○○○○○○○○○○○○○○

DATE:	WEEK:	WEIGHT:

Warm Up/ Stretching   **Duration:**

Exercise		Set 1	Set 2	Set 3	Set 4	Set 5
	Weight					
	Reps					
	Weight					
	Reps					
	Weight					
	Reps					
	Weight					
	Reps					
	Weight					
	Reps					
	Weight					
	Reps					
	Weight					
	Reps					
	Weight					
	Reps					
	Weight					
	Reps					
	Weight					
	Reps					
	Weight					
	Reps					
	Weight					
	Reps					

CARDIO WORKOUT

Exercise	Duration	Pace	Heart Rate	Calories

WATER   1 cup per circle
(1 cup = 8 ounces ~ 240ml)   ○○○○○○○○○○○○○○○○○○

DATE:	WEEK:	WEIGHT:

Warm Up/ Stretching					Duration:	

Exercise		Set 1	Set 2	Set 3	Set 4	Set 5
	Weight					
	Reps					
	Weight					
	Reps					
	Weight					
	Reps					
	Weight					
	Reps					
	Weight					
	Reps					
	Weight					
	Reps					
	Weight					
	Reps					
	Weight					
	Reps					
	Weight					
	Reps					
	Weight					
	Reps					
	Weight					
	Reps					
	Weight					
	Reps					
	Weight					
	Reps					

CARDIO WORKOUT

Exercise	Duration	Pace	Heart Rate	Calories

WATER   1 cup per circle
(1 cup = 8 ounces ~ 240ml)   ○○○○○○○○○○○○○○○○

DATE: **WEEK:**   **WEIGHT:**

Warm Up/ Stretching   **Duration:**

Exercise		Set 1	Set 2	Set 3	Set 4	Set 5
	Weight					
	Reps					
	Weight					
	Reps					
	Weight					
	Reps					
	Weight					
	Reps					
	Weight					
	Reps					
	Weight					
	Reps					
	Weight					
	Reps					
	Weight					
	Reps					
	Weight					
	Reps					
	Weight					
	Reps					
	Weight					
	Reps					
	Weight					
	Reps					

CARDIO WORKOUT

Exercise	Duration	Pace	Heart Rate	Calories

WATER   1 cup per circle
(1 cup = 8 ounces ~ 240ml)   ○○○○○○○○○○○○○○○○○○

DATE:	WEEK:	WEIGHT:

Warm Up/ Stretching	Duration:

Exercise		Set 1	Set 2	Set 3	Set 4	Set 5
	Weight					
	Reps					
	Weight					
	Reps					
	Weight					
	Reps					
	Weight					
	Reps					
	Weight					
	Reps					
	Weight					
	Reps					
	Weight					
	Reps					
	Weight					
	Reps					
	Weight					
	Reps					
	Weight					
	Reps					
	Weight					
	Reps					
	Weight					
	Reps					

CARDIO WORKOUT

Exercise	Duration	Pace	Heart Rate	Calories

WATER   1 cup per circle
(1 cup = 8 ounces ~ 240ml)   ◯◯◯◯◯◯◯◯◯◯◯◯◯◯◯◯

DATE: **WEEK:** **WEIGHT:**

Warm Up/ Stretching **Duration:**

Exercise		Set 1	Set 2	Set 3	Set 4	Set 5
	Weight					
	Reps					
	Weight					
	Reps					
	Weight					
	Reps					
	Weight					
	Reps					
	Weight					
	Reps					
	Weight					
	Reps					
	Weight					
	Reps					
	Weight					
	Reps					
	Weight					
	Reps					
	Weight					
	Reps					
	Weight					
	Reps					
	Weight					
	Reps					

CARDIO WORKOUT

Exercise	Duration	Pace	Heart Rate	Calories

WATER 1 cup per circle
(1 cup = 8 ounces ~ 240ml) ○○○○○○○○○○○○○○○○○○

DATE:		WEEK:		WEIGHT:	

Warm Up/ Stretching   Duration:

Exercise		Set 1	Set 2	Set 3	Set 4	Set 5
	Weight					
	Reps					
	Weight					
	Reps					
	Weight					
	Reps					
	Weight					
	Reps					
	Weight					
	Reps					
	Weight					
	Reps					
	Weight					
	Reps					
	Weight					
	Reps					
	Weight					
	Reps					
	Weight					
	Reps					
	Weight					
	Reps					
	Weight					
	Reps					

CARDIO WORKOUT

Exercise	Duration	Pace	Heart Rate	Calories

WATER   1 cup per circle
(1 cup = 8 ounces ~ 240ml)   ○○○○○○○○○○○○○○○○○

DATE: | **WEEK:** | **WEIGHT:**

Warm Up/ Stretching   Duration:

Exercise		Set 1	Set 2	Set 3	Set 4	Set 5
	Weight					
	Reps					
	Weight					
	Reps					
	Weight					
	Reps					
	Weight					
	Reps					
	Weight					
	Reps					
	Weight					
	Reps					
	Weight					
	Reps					
	Weight					
	Reps					
	Weight					
	Reps					
	Weight					
	Reps					
	Weight					
	Reps					
	Weight					
	Reps					

CARDIO WORKOUT

Exercise	Duration	Pace	Heart Rate	Calories

WATER   1 cup per circle
(1 cup = 8 ounces ~ 240ml)   ◯◯◯◯◯◯◯◯◯◯◯◯◯◯◯◯◯

DATE:	WEEK:	WEIGHT:

Warm Up/ Stretching   **Duration:**

Exercise		Set 1	Set 2	Set 3	Set 4	Set 5
	Weight					
	Reps					
	Weight					
	Reps					
	Weight					
	Reps					
	Weight					
	Reps					
	Weight					
	Reps					
	Weight					
	Reps					
	Weight					
	Reps					
	Weight					
	Reps					
	Weight					
	Reps					
	Weight					
	Reps					
	Weight					
	Reps					
	Weight					
	Reps					

CARDIO WORKOUT

Exercise	Duration	Pace	Heart Rate	Calories

WATER   1 cup per circle
(1 cup = 8 ounces ~ 240ml)   ○ ○ ○ ○ ○ ○ ○ ○ ○ ○ ○ ○ ○ ○ ○ ○

DATE:	WEEK:	WEIGHT:

Warm Up/ Stretching Duration:

Exercise		Set 1	Set 2	Set 3	Set 4	Set 5
	Weight					
	Reps					
	Weight					
	Reps					
	Weight					
	Reps					
	Weight					
	Reps					
	Weight					
	Reps					
	Weight					
	Reps					
	Weight					
	Reps					
	Weight					
	Reps					
	Weight					
	Reps					
	Weight					
	Reps					
	Weight					
	Reps					
	Weight					
	Reps					

CARDIO WORKOUT

Exercise	Duration	Pace	Heart Rate	Calories

WATER   1 cup per circle
(1 cup = 8 ounces ~ 240ml)   ○○○○○○○○○○○○○○○○○○

DATE:	WEEK:	WEIGHT:

Warm Up/ Stretching	Duration:

Exercise		Set 1	Set 2	Set 3	Set 4	Set 5
	Weight					
	Reps					
	Weight					
	Reps					
	Weight					
	Reps					
	Weight					
	Reps					
	Weight					
	Reps					
	Weight					
	Reps					
	Weight					
	Reps					
	Weight					
	Reps					
	Weight					
	Reps					
	Weight					
	Reps					
	Weight					
	Reps					
	Weight					
	Reps					

CARDIO WORKOUT

Exercise	Duration	Pace	Heart Rate	Calories

WATER   1 cup per circle
(1 cup = 8 ounces ~ 240ml)   ○○○○○○○○○○○○○○○

DATE:	WEEK:	WEIGHT:

Warm Up/ Stretching   Duration:

Exercise		Set 1	Set 2	Set 3	Set 4	Set 5
	Weight					
	Reps					
	Weight					
	Reps					
	Weight					
	Reps					
	Weight					
	Reps					
	Weight					
	Reps					
	Weight					
	Reps					
	Weight					
	Reps					
	Weight					
	Reps					
	Weight					
	Reps					
	Weight					
	Reps					
	Weight					
	Reps					
	Weight					
	Reps					
	Weight					
	Reps					

CARDIO WORKOUT

Exercise	Duration	Pace	Heart Rate	Calories

WATER   1 cup per circle
(1 cup = 8 ounces ~ 240ml)   ○○○○○○○○○○○○○○○○○○

DATE:	WEEK:	WEIGHT:

Warm Up/ Stretching　　　　　　　　　　　　Duration:

Exercise		Set 1	Set 2	Set 3	Set 4	Set 5
	Weight					
	Reps					
	Weight					
	Reps					
	Weight					
	Reps					
	Weight					
	Reps					
	Weight					
	Reps					
	Weight					
	Reps					
	Weight					
	Reps					
	Weight					
	Reps					
	Weight					
	Reps					
	Weight					
	Reps					
	Weight					
	Reps					
	Weight					
	Reps					

CARDIO WORKOUT

Exercise	Duration	Pace	Heart Rate	Calories

WATER   1 cup per circle
(1 cup = 8 ounces ~ 240ml)   ○○○○○○○○○○○○○○○○

Printed in Great Britain
by Amazon

34531449R00068